Invisible
EXPOSURE
The Science of **Ultraviolet Rays**

HEADLINE SCIENCE

by Darlene R. Stille

Content Adviser:
Douglas E. Brash, Ph.D.
Professor of Therapeutic Radiology, Genetics,
and Dermatology, Yale School of Medicine

Science Adviser:
Terrence E. Young Jr., M.Ed., M.L.S.,
Jefferson Parish (Louisiana) Public School System

Reading Adviser:
Alexa L. Sandmann, Ed.D., Professor of Literacy
College and Graduate School of Education, Health,
and Human Services, Kent State University

COMPASS POINT BOOKS
a capstone imprint

Compass Point Books • 151 Good Counsel Drive, P. O. Box 669 • Mankato, MN 56002-0669

This book was manufactured with paper containing
at least 10 percent post-consumer waste.

Library of Congress Cataloging-in-Publication Data
Stille, Darlene R.
  Invisible exposure : the science of ultraviolet rays / by Darlene R.
  Stille ; illustrator, Farhana Hossain.
    p. cm.—(Headline science)
  Includes index.
  ISBN 978-0-7565-4215-3 (library binding)
  1. Ultraviolet radiation—Juvenile literature. I. Hossain, Farhana,
ill. II. Title. III. Series.

  QC459.S75 2010
  535.01'4—dc22   2009033569

Editor: Anthony Wacholtz
Designer: Ted Williams
Photo Researcher: Svetlana Zhurkin
Illustrator: Farhana Hossain
Production Specialist: Jane Klenk

Photographs ©: Photographs ©: Capstone Studio/Karon Dubke, 29; EyeWire, 12; Getty Images/3D4Medical, 41,
China Photos, 43, Nucleus Medical Art, 26; iStockphoto/Carmen Martínez, 27, David Newton, 42, Eileen Hart,
cover (inset, middle), 25, Joe_Potato, 40, Nickos, 33, Tammy Bryngelson, 13, tillsonburg, 17; NASA, 8, image cour-
tesy Jeff Schmaltz, MODIS Land Rapid Response Team at NASA GSFC, 34, ESA, M. Robberto (Space Telescope Science Institute/ESA) and the Hubble Space Telescope Orion Treasury Project Team, 9; National Cancer Institute,
20, 22; NOAA, 31, NOS/ORR/Dr. Robert Ricker, 35; Peter Arnold/Zeva Oelbaum, 21; Photodisc, 5; Shutterstock/
Biczó Zsolt, cover (bottom), Elena Elisseeva, 23, EuToch, 28, Gareth Trevor, 32, Ivanagott, 7, Lynne Furrer, 15, Shane
White, cover (inset, right), 11, Vidux, 14; SOHO (ESA & NASA), cover (inset, left), 38; Svetlana Zhurkin, 16; Visuals
Unlimited/Dr. David Phillips, 19; Wikimedia/Newbie, 39.

Visit Compass Point Books on the Internet at *www.compasspointbooks.com*
or e-mail your request to *custserv@compasspointbooks.com*

Chapter 1
Sunburns and
Rainbows
Page 4

Chapter 2
Dangers to
the Skin
Page 10

Chapter 3
UV Rays
and Cancer
Page 18

Chapter 4
Eye-Damaging
UV Rays
Page 24

Chapter 5
The Ozone Layer
and UV Rays
Page 30

Chapter 6
Useful UV Rays
Page 37

Timeline   Page 44
Glossary   Page 45
Further Resources   Page 46
Source Notes   Page 47
Index   Page 48

NV TOWN POSTS SIGNAL TO WARN ABOUT UV RAYS

The Mercury News, San Jose, California
November 28, 2008

It may look like a traffic light, but the purpose of a new signal along U.S. 395 in Gardnerville [Nevada] is to warn the public about the sun's ultraviolet radiation.

The St. Gall Knights of Columbus ... paid for the $2,195 signal that measures how much sun protection is needed to be outdoors. The light ranges from low green when it's safe outside with proper sun protection to violet when it's unsafe to be outside.

Knights council members say the sign near the town's maintenance yard is designed to encourage local youth to take preventative measures.

Just as traffic lights are meant to prevent accidents, a light in Nevada warns people about dangerous ultraviolet rays. More than a dozen members of the St. Gall Knights of Columbus have needed medical treatment for damage to their skin caused by UV rays. People in Gardnerville are especially susceptible to these rays because the town lies about 4,750 feet (1,450 meters) above sea level. Government officials in other sun-drenched areas may install warning lights as well.

DANGEROUS RAYS

UV radiation comes from the sun and is invisible. These rays can be very dangerous. They can cause sunburn, cancer, and other types of damage to your skin.

People enjoy spending time outside on a sunny day, but they may not realize UV rays from the sun can be dangerous without proper protection.

News changes every minute, and readers need access to the latest information to keep current. Here are a few key search terms to help you locate up-to-the-minute UV rays headlines:

fluorescent lighting UV rays

ozone UV rays

melanoma

The Skin Cancer Foundation

NASA UV rays

Sun Protection Factor

NOAA UV rays

UV Index

Ultraviolet radiation is a small part of a much bigger radiation "family." Rainbows also belong to the family. Rainbows are made up of visible light, and visible light contains all colors. Ordinarily your eyes do not see all the individual colors at the same time. When all colors are together, the light looks white.

In the late 1600s, English scientist Sir Isaac Newton learned about the colors in white light. He studied light passing through a prism—a glass object that has several flat sides cut at angles. A prism can split visible light into all colors. Raindrops can do the same thing, and that's how rainbows are created. This works because light is a form of energy, and energy behaves like waves.

Visible light is made up of waves of various lengths. The length of a wave is the distance between the wave's crests (highest points). When white light passes through a prism or raindrop, its waves bend. Because

HEADLINE
SCIENCE

each color bends differently, the colors in the beam of light separate. Your eyes see the light as a band of individual colors.

Each wavelength bends at a different angle. For example, the longest wavelength of visible light bends the least when it passes through a prism or a raindrop. This wave appears as red light. The shortest wavelength of visible light bends the most, creating violet light.

The human eye cannot see colors beyond the ends of the rainbow. But there are invisible waves of energy out there. Beyond red are longer wavelengths of infrared radiation. Beyond violet are shorter wavelengths of ultraviolet radiation.

Just as light of differing wavelengths forms the colors of the rainbow, other energy with differing wavelengths forms various types of ultraviolet radiation. The UV rays with the longest wavelengths are called UVA rays. UVB rays are shorter, followed by the shortest: UVC rays. Only UVA and UVB rays reach Earth.

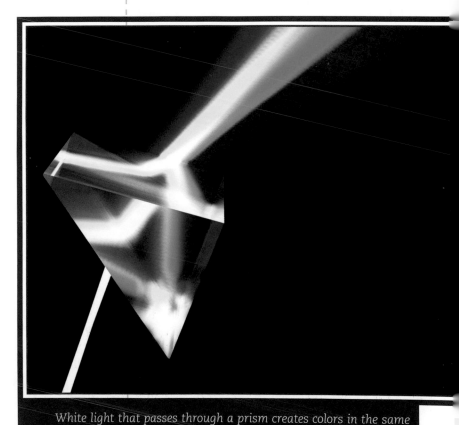

White light that passes through a prism creates colors in the same order every time: red, orange, yellow, green, blue, indigo, and violet.

NOW YOU KNOW

Bees can detect mixes of ultraviolet, blue, and green. With ultraviolet light, bees can see patterns on flowers that aren't visible in ordinary white light. The patterns help the insects find nectar and pollinate the flowers.

WHERE UV RAYS COME FROM

Visible light and UV rays are forms of electromagnetic energy. Radio waves, X-rays, and microwaves also belong to this big family of electromagnetic radiation. They are all related to light. What makes an X-ray or a radio wave different from visible light or ultraviolet rays is the lengths of their waves. You can think of them as part of the "rainbow" of waves that make up the electromagnetic spectrum.

Radio waves and microwaves,

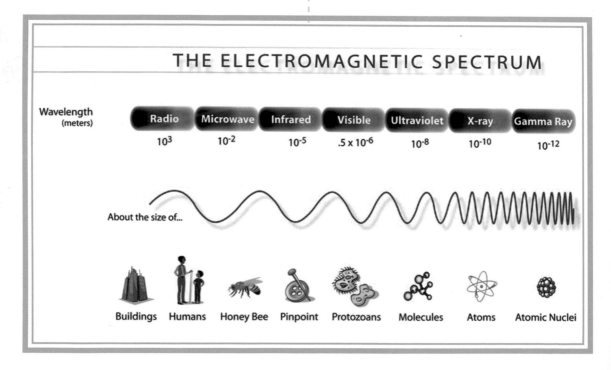

THE ELECTROMAGNETIC SPECTRUM

Wavelength (meters)	Radio	Microwave	Infrared	Visible	Ultraviolet	X-ray	Gamma Ray
	10^3	10^{-2}	10^{-5}	$.5 \times 10^{-6}$	10^{-8}	10^{-10}	10^{-12}
About the size of...	Buildings	Humans	Honey Bee	Pinpoint	Protozoans	Molecules	Atoms	Atomic Nuclei

Gas and dust from the Orion Nebula form new, massive stars. These stars emit powerful ultraviolet light.

at one end of the spectrum, have extremely long wavelengths. Some radio waves can stretch for more than 6,214 miles (10,000 km). That's about twice as far as the United States is wide. At the other end of the spectrum are short waves that include X-rays and gamma rays. Gamma ray wavelengths are less than 10-trillionths of a meter—much smaller than an atom.

Natural UV rays on Earth come from the sun. UV rays can also come from distant stars and other objects in the universe. Artificial UV rays can be created by passing an electric current through certain gases in sealed tubes. The current causes changes in the gas atoms, which produces UV rays.

CONFUSED BY SPF? TAKE A NUMBER

The New York Times
May 13, 2009

SPF ... has hit the triple digits ... leading some dermatologists to complain that this is merely a numbers game that confuses consumers. The parade of stratospheric SPFs is "crazy," said Dr. Barbara A. Gilchrest, a dermatology professor at Boston University School of Medicine.

A sunscreen's SPF, or sun protection factor, measures how much the product shields the sun's shorter-wave ultraviolet B rays, known as UVB radiation, which can cause sunburn. It used to be that SPF topped out at 30. No more. These days, a race is on among sunscreen makers to create the highest SPF that [research and development] can buy.

Knowing which sunscreen to use can be confusing. Some experts think that sunscreens aren't as effective as they should be. Other experts say a more effective sunscreen is not needed. Most experts agree, however, that using sunscreen is important. They also agree that it should be put on often.

SOAKING UP RAYS

Soaking up rays is more than just a casual term for sunbathing. It is a good description of what happens when ultraviolet rays strike the skin. When electromagnetic rays strike a material, they either enter the material or are stopped. UVA and UVB rays enter the skin. Then they start to

Areas of the skin exposed to the sun will turn red and may become painful to the touch if sunscreen isn't used.

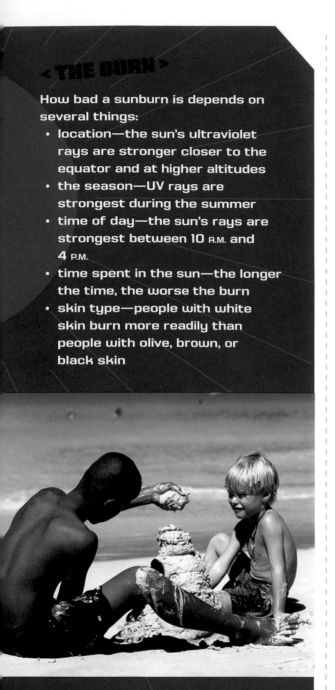

< THE BURN >

How bad a sunburn is depends on several things:

- location—the sun's ultraviolet rays are stronger closer to the equator and at higher altitudes
- the season—UV rays are strongest during the summer
- time of day—the sun's rays are strongest between 10 A.M. and 4 P.M.
- time spent in the sun—the longer the time, the worse the burn
- skin type—people with white skin burn more readily than people with olive, brown, or black skin

cause problems—from sunburn and wrinkles to skin cancer.

UVA rays, with the longest UV wavelength, go deeper into the skin than UVB rays. The shorter UVB rays do not go as deep, but they are more powerful and can burn the skin more quickly. Both UV rays can cause tanning.

THE BURNING RAYS

Skin has three layers, and UVB rays can burn all three. The outer layer of skin is called the epidermis. It is as thin as a sheet of paper. The middle layer, the dermis, is up to 40 times as thick as the epidermis. It contains nerves and blood vessels. The innermost layer is called the subcutaneous tissue. This is a thick layer that contains fat cells.

UVB rays kill skin cells. The body then sends blood to the skin surface. Red blood cells make the sunburned skin look red. The blood also carries white blood cells to clean up the dead skin cells.

The mildest sunburn—a first-degree sunburn—causes only red,

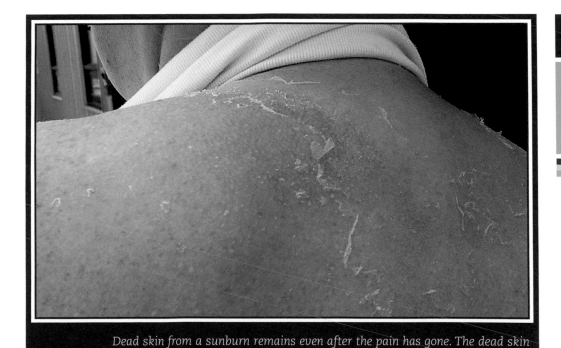

Dead skin from a sunburn remains even after the pain has gone. The dead skin eventually falls off, a process called peeling, as it is replaced with new skin.

HEADLINE SCIENCE

painful areas on the epidermis. If UVB rays damage the dermis, the skin gets red, and water-filled blisters form. This type of burn is a second-degree sunburn. A very serious third-degree sunburn results if UVB rays burn down into the subcutaneous layer. In addition to blisters, the skin can look raw. Third-degree sunburn must be treated by a doctor to prevent infection and loss of body fluids.

THE TANNING RAYS

More UVA rays travel to Earth than any other kind of radiation from the sun. During the day, UVA rays are all around. UVA rays can travel through clouds and through ordinary window glass.

While UVB rays kill skin cells on the upper epidermis, UVA rays reach deeper, to cells called melanocytes. UVA rays cause the melanocytes to make a dark pigment. This colored substance, melanin, absorbs UV rays.

As the cells make more melanin, the skin turns darker.

This tanning protects against sunburn. Many people who stay in the sun for short periods of time every day build up a tan. Their skin gets darker and takes longer to burn. Some people think that tanned skin has a healthy look. Dermatologists, however, say there is no such thing as a healthy tan. Tanning is a sure sign of ultraviolet damage to the skin. Tanning is just the body's way of trying to limit that damage.

Tanning gives some protection against sunburn, but it does not protect people from other UV dangers. Ultraviolet light causes skin to look old, leathery, and wrinkled. It can cause dark blotches called liver spots or age spots. Sometimes scaly patches called actinic keratoses appear. UV rays also cause damage that can lead to skin cancer, which can be deadly.

< ARTIFICIAL TAN >

Indoor tanning beds, also called sunbeds, make artificial UV rays so people can get tans year-round. Indoor tanning has become especially popular among teenage girls. Some tanning bed makers say their product gives off mainly harmless UVA rays. Dermatologists warn, however, that tanning beds are not safe. UV rays from tanning beds can cause sunburn and skin damage, including cancer. As a result, California, Texas, New Jersey, and more than 20 other states have laws that limit teenagers' use of this equipment.

Although age spots are most common for people over the age of 40, they can appear on the skin of younger people as well.

SUNSCREENS AND SUNBLOCKS

Many people rub or spray a sunblock or a sunscreen on their skin. Sunblocks contain the chemical compounds zinc oxide and titanium dioxide, which create a white film on the skin. The film is very good at blocking UVA and UVB rays.

Sunscreens contain chemicals that absorb UV rays. Some absorb UVA, and others absorb UVB. Many sunscreens contain both types of chemicals. Dermatologists recommend choosing sunscreens labeled "broad spectrum" to get both UVA and UVB protection. Sunscreens are less visible on the skin than sunblocks, but they can lose their ability to protect after a few hours. Be sure to check the label to see how often your sunscreen needs to be applied.

NOW YOU KNOW

You are not safe from sunburn on an overcast day. UV rays may be less intense, but they can go through clouds. UV rays can even reach you when you swim, because the rays can pass through water.

The SPF (sun protection factor) numbers on sunscreens show how much protection they give against burning UVB rays. In general, the numbers tell you how long you can stay in the sun without getting burned. An SPF of 15, for example, means that you can stay in the sun 15 times as long as you could without protection.

Suppose you normally burn after 15 minutes in the sun. Sunscreen

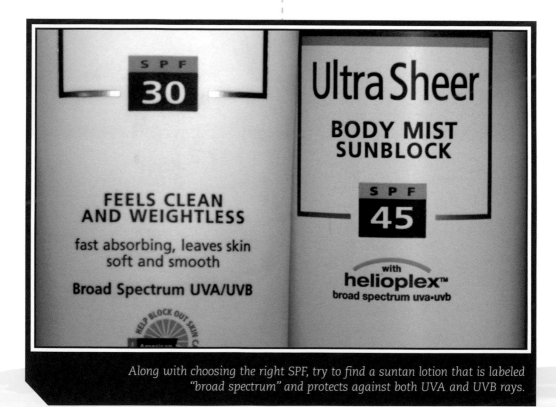

Along with choosing the right SPF, try to find a suntan lotion that is labeled "broad spectrum" and protects against both UVA and UVB rays.

with an SPF of 15 would let you sunbathe for 225 minutes, or about 3 hours and 45 minutes. But use SPF numbers carefully. They are only accurate if plenty of sunscreen is on all exposed skin, and if you put on more as often as the label suggests. And remember that some sunlight gets through the sunscreen anyway.

Not everyone agrees on how accurate SPF numbers are in describing UVB protection. Some sunscreens have ratings as high as SPF 60. Some dermatologists are especially concerned about the accuracy of any rating above SPF 30. The FDA recommends using a sunscreen with a rating of at least SPF 15, but it also wants to limit the highest SPF to a rating of 30+. Dermatologists fear that using sunscreens with high SPF ratings encourages people to stay

Sunscreen should be applied to any part of your skin that may be exposed to the sun.

in the sun long enough to damage their skin. They also know that many sunbathers apply too little sunscreen, especially since it can come off in the water while swimming. You need to put on two to four tablespoons (30 to 60 milliliters) of sunscreen to get the best protection.

TANNING BEDS AS CARCINOGENIC AS ASBESTOS AND CIGARETTES

Los Angeles Times
July 28, 2009

The ultraviolet light used in tanning beds is as carcinogenic as asbestos, arsenic, radium and cigarettes, a special committee of the World Health Organization's International Agency for Research on Cancer has concluded. ...

Moreover, the committee concluded that all types of UV radiation induce cancer, not just [UV-B rays]. Some tanning salons claim to use only UV-A, which was thought to be safer, but the committee said that is not the case.

The committee of 20 scientists from nine countries met in June and reviewed more than 20 studies in humans, as well as animal studies. They reported online in the journal *Lancet Oncology* that the risk of skin cancer increases 75% when people start using tanning beds before age 30.

The U.S. government considers ultra-violet radiation of all types to be a carcinogen. A carcinogen creates changes in cells that lead to cancer—an uncontrolled growth of cells.

Normal cells divide, grow, and then die. New cells replace the dead ones. Cell division and cell death are important in the skin.

For example, at the bottom of the epidermis, basal cells divide to form new cells. New cells formed by division are called daughter cells. Some of these daughter cells make their way toward the skin surface. Near the surface of the epidermis, the cells die. They form the dry outer layer of the skin that protects everything inside the body. Eventually the dead cells flake off. New skin cells constantly form to replace the dead skin cells.

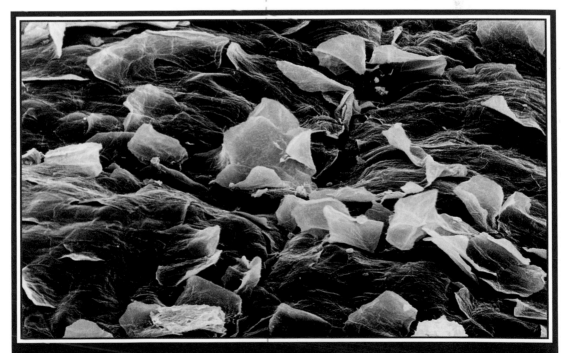

Skin cells known as epithelial cells die and fall off to make room for new cells. In humans, skin cells are replaced every 35 days.

Sometimes there are problems with this orderly routine. A cell might not die. Instead it begins to divide over and over again. The wildly dividing cells become a lump of cells called a tumor, which can be benign or cancerous. A benign tumor does not spread, but a cancerous tumor can spread. Cancerous cells can break away from the tumor and travel through the bloodstream. The traveling cells can start new cancerous tumors in other parts of the body. As cancerous tumors grow, they can prevent organs, such as the brain, liver, or kidneys, from working correctly.

Changes that lead to cancer begin in a cell's DNA—the molecule that genes are made of. DNA controls everything that happens in cells, including when they start and stop dividing. Ultraviolet rays that penetrate a skin cell damage part of the DNA molecule. The rays can cause mutations (changes) in the DNA. The rays could, for example, disrupt the DNA switches that turn cell division on and off. If this happens, the cell can become cancerous.

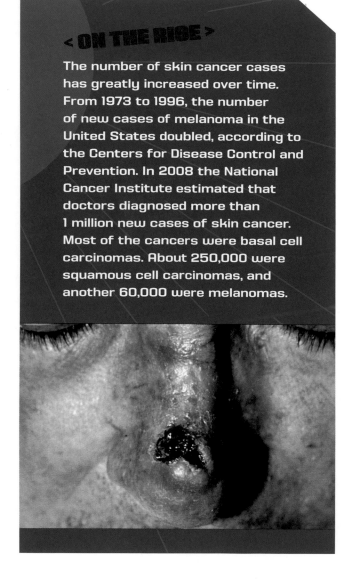

< ON THE RISE >

The number of skin cancer cases has greatly increased over time. From 1973 to 1996, the number of new cases of melanoma in the United States doubled, according to the Centers for Disease Control and Prevention. In 2008 the National Cancer Institute estimated that doctors diagnosed more than 1 million new cases of skin cancer. Most of the cancers were basal cell carcinomas. About 250,000 were squamous cell carcinomas, and another 60,000 were melanomas.

COMMON SKIN CANCERS

Basal cell cancer is the most common type of cancer. It accounts for about 75 percent of all skin cancers in the United States, according to the American Cancer Society. This cancer starts in hair follicle cells that divide to form new skin and hair cells. The cancer can look like a sore, a bump, or even a dip in the skin. Basal cell cancer grows slowly and rarely spreads elsewhere in the body.

Doctors usually remove these cancers through surgery.

Squamous cell cancer is another common skin cancer. It begins in the epidermis-producing cells that lie between hair follicles. It grows faster than basal cell cancer. A growing bump that looks like a wart or a red patch on the skin may be a sign of this cancer. It can spread to other parts of the body, so this cancer should be removed surgically as soon as it is found.

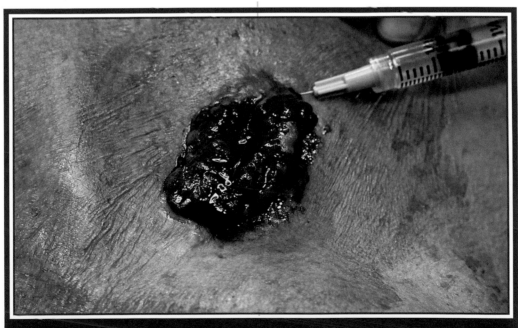

About 95 percent of people with squamous cell cancer can be cured if the growths are removed quickly. If left for too long, the cancerous cells could spread.

DEADLY MELANOMA

Melanoma is a rarer form of skin cancer, but it is also the most dangerous skin cancer. Melanoma begins in the melanocytes. Melanomas can start as moles that change color or shape. They can also start as new moles.

If not removed, melanomas grow down toward the blood vessels. Blood can carry these cancerous cells to other parts of the body. Melanomas need to be removed before they reach the bloodstream. Melanoma can be deadly if it spreads to other parts of the body. Melanomas are treated with surgery and sometimes also with chemotherapy and radiation.

HOW TO PROTECT YOURSELF

There are several steps you can take to protect against ultraviolet radiation. You can remain indoors during the hours of most intense sunshine, from 10 A.M. to 4 P.M. If you are outdoors during these

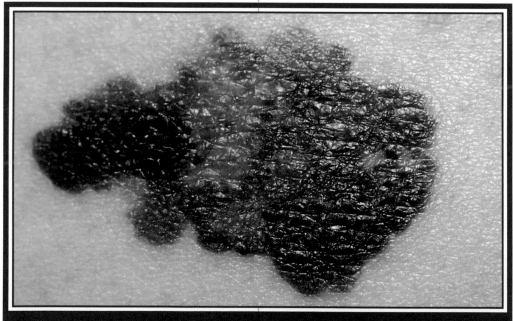

Most melanomas are dark colored. If a mole is more than ¼ inch (6 millimeters) in diameter, it is more likely to be a melanoma.

Wearing a wide-brimmed hat on a sunny day can help shield your face from ultraviolet rays.

NOW YOU KNOW

"Slip! Slop! Slap!" is a slogan created by a government organization in Australia. It reminds people how to protect against UV rays. It stands for: Slip on a shirt. Slop on sunscreen. Slap on a hat.

hours, try to stay in shady areas.

Regardless of the time of day, it's important to cover up when you're in sunlight. A wide-brimmed hat is good protection for your scalp and face. Long sleeves and long pants will cover up your arms and legs. Chemically treated shirts, T-shirts, and other clothing that block UV rays are available. You can also use a sunscreen or sunblock with SPF 15 or greater.

CHILDREN SHOULD WEAR SUNGLASSES WHEN OUTSIDE

>>> *Sun Sentinel*, Fort Lauderdale, Florida
July 22, 2009

The long-term effects of excessive sunlight aren't seen early in life—they show up when people are 60 or 70 years old ... says Steven Schiff, an optometrist in Deer Park, N.Y. Just as parents want to protect their children from skin cancer by putting sunscreen on them, parents should protect children's eyes by getting them in the habit of wearing sunglasses outdoors.

Most sunglasses labeled 100 percent UV protection, and preferably 100 percent both UVA and UVB protection, are the best bet. One mistake parents make is having children don the shades only when they are going to the beach. If a child is outside playing sports or at a park, the eyes should be protected then as well, Schiff says.

How do they look? That may be the first thing a teen thinks about when buying sunglasses. It would be a good idea, however, to think more about blocking out UV rays.

Invisible UV rays can enter the eye along with visible light. Eyes need visible light to see. Eyes, however, do not actually see objects. They detect the light reflected off the objects and send this information to the brain.

UV rays, along with rays of ordinary light, enter your eye through the cornea, a tough, clear covering over the eye. The rays travel to a colored circle called the iris. An opening in the center of the iris, the pupil, grows larger or smaller to control how much light enters your eye.

Behind the iris and pupil is a clear lens that focuses the light to create an image. The lens directs

The key to picking sunglasses is how much protection they provide against UV rays.

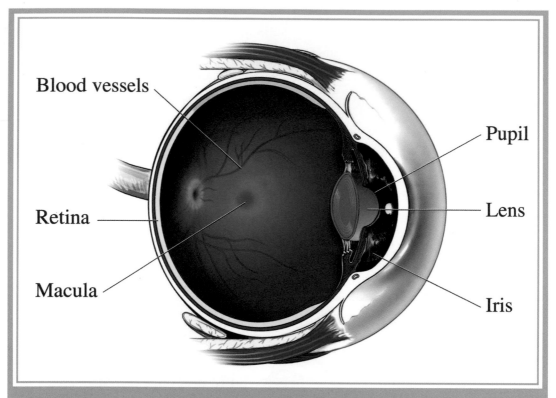

Blood vessels

Retina

Macula

Pupil

Lens

Iris

Each part of the eye has a specific purpose. For example, the macula helps us see things in detail and allows us to focus when we read.

the focused light to the retina at the back of the eye. The retina is thin and delicate, but it contains many special light-detecting cells. These cells, called rods and cones, change visible light into electrical signals. The signals travel over nerves to your brain. Your brain then "sees" all the objects around you.

EYES CAN GET SUNBURNED

It is important to keep UV rays from damaging the delicate retina. One job of the cornea and the lens is to act as natural sunglasses and block UV rays. The problem is that UV rays can damage these eye parts, too.

The cornea can suffer a sunburn from UVB rays after just one day on the beach without sunglasses. The sun's rays are especially strong at the beach, because they reflect off the sand and water.

The cornea can get sunburned easily on snowy ski slopes as well. The sun's rays reflect strongly off snow just as they do off sand or water. One name for a sunburned cornea is snow blindness, but the scientific name is photokeratitis. It is quite painful. Symptoms of photokeratitis include redness, lots of tears, and a gritty feeling in the eyes. After several days, the sunburned cornea usually heals itself.

Eyes that are repeatedly exposed to strong UV rays can suffer serious problems. Medical scientists think UV radiation may be one reason eyes develop cataracts. Cataracts are cloudy

Wearing wrap-around sunglasses or goggles is the best way to protect your eyes when hitting the slopes.

places in the lens of the eye, and they are most common among older people. Cataracts make seeing difficult, but they can be removed with surgery.

UV rays can also lead to growths in and around eyes. Noncancerous growths can form in the corner of the eye. If these growths block vision, they might have to be removed by a surgeon. Basal cell and squamous cell cancers can form on eyelids, and melanomas can form inside the eye.

CHOOSING THE RIGHT SUNGLASSES

A good pair of sunglasses goes a long way toward protecting your eyes. The sunglass lenses may be either glass or plastic. A special film applied over the lenses provides UV protection.

Look for a label that says the glasses block 99 to 100 percent of both UVA and UVB radiation. Regular eyeglasses and contact lenses can also be coated to provide UV protection.

Most eye doctors say lens color does not matter in terms of blocking UV rays. Many people like gray or green lenses because they can see colors better with them. Skiers like

Sunglasses that offer UV protection come in a wide variety of styles and colors.

< EYE COLOR >

Melanin made by melanocytes in the iris is what gives eyes their color. The more melanin a person has, the darker his or her eyes will be. People with blue or green eyes have less melanin in their irises than people with brown eyes. People with light-colored eyes usually have light-colored skin and have a greater chance of developing skin or eye cancer.

The melanin in the eyes of some people is distributed unevenly, creating two different colors in the irises. In some cases, the left eye is a different color from the right eye. Some people have two colors in the same eye.

HEADLINE SCIENCE

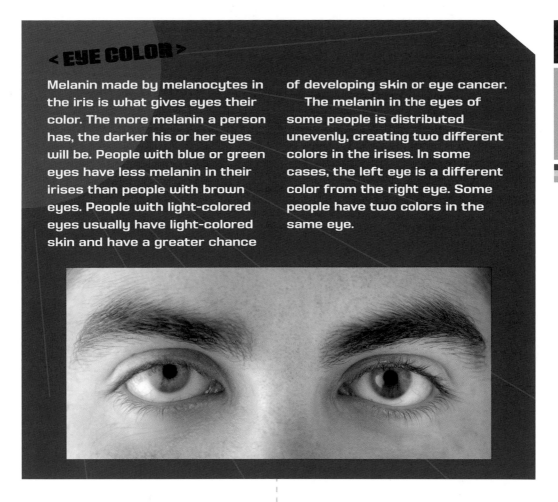

amber-colored lenses, which block blue light rays. These "blue-blockers" make surroundings look sharper. It's important not to be fooled by how dark the lenses are. Darkness has no effect on how good the lenses are at blocking out UV rays.

There are other reasons why you should wear sunglasses. Wearing wrap-around sunglasses will protect the sides of your eyes. Use sunglasses even if you have UV-protected contact lenses. Contact lenses do not cover your entire eye or your eyelids. For extra eye protection, wear a visor or a hat with a brim.

CHEMICALS THAT EASED ONE WOE WORSEN ANOTHER

The Washington Post
July 20, 2009

Scientists say the chemicals that helped solve the last global environmental crisis—the hole in the ozone layer—are making the current one worse. The chemicals, called hydrofluorocarbons (HFCs), were introduced widely in the 1990s to replace [CFCs] used in air conditioners, refrigerators and insulating foam.

They worked: The earth's protective shield seems to be recovering. But researchers say what's good for ozone is bad for climate change. In the atmosphere, [HFCs] act like "super" greenhouse gases, with a heat-trapping power that can be 4,470 times that of carbon dioxide. Now, scientists say, the world must find replacements for the replacements—or these super-emissions could cancel out other efforts to stop global warming.

Among other science groups, the German Aerospace Center keeps track of the size of the ozone hole from year to year. Changing temperatures and wind directions in Antarctica cause the hole to grow and shrink throughout the year. The coldest months in Antarctica are from April to August. Because the South Pole is tipped away from the sun then, Antarctica receives very little sunlight during those months. A powerful wind keeps warmer air from coming southward to Antarctica. This means the ozone hole grows during these cold months.

DAMAGING THE OZONE LAYER

Ozone is a gas high in Earth's atmosphere—a blanket of gases that surrounds the planet. Ozone is made of oxygen. Ultraviolet rays break molecules of oxygen in the atmosphere into two oxygen atoms. The atoms join unbroken oxygen molecules, creating ozone. Oxygen molecules have two oxygen atoms (O_2). Ozone molecules are made of three oxygen atoms (O_3).

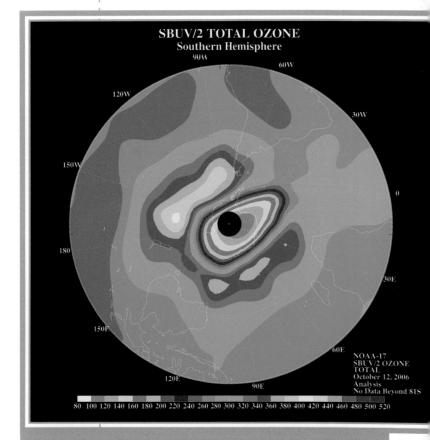

A National Oceanic and Atmospheric Administration satellite image indicates the ozone layer is thinning in several areas in the Southern Hemisphere.

The ozone that the ultraviolet rays create protects life on Earth from UV damage. It keeps about 99 percent of the sun's UV radiation from reaching Earth. Without the ozone layer, life could not exist.

Scientists studying the atmosphere first noticed a problem with the ozone layer in the late 1970s and early 1980s. They found that the number of ozone molecules in the layer over Antarctica was decreasing. Researchers discovered that industrial chemicals called chlorofluorocarbons were destroying the ozone. CFCs were used in the cooling parts of refrigerators and air conditioners and in spray cans. The CFCs made their way into the atmosphere and settled on cold ice clouds over Antarctica. UV rays broke the CFCs into smaller molecules that changed the ozone into ordinary

Three billion aerosol cans are produced in the United States each year, but they no longer contain CFCs.

A CFC recovery area in Oxfordshire, England, was set up to allow people to drop off refrigerators and freezers that use CFCs. The appliances are then properly disposed.

oxygen, which doesn't block UV rays. A smaller ozone hole also formed over the Arctic.

Most nations banned the use of CFCs by the mid-1990s. But CFCs are not going away quickly. Some CFCs can last in the atmosphere for up to 100 years. During this time, they will continue to damage the ozone layer.

Scientists and manufacturers turned to the use of hydrofluoro-carbons, which have been shown to help the ozone layer. They soon discovered, though, that the HFCs were trapping much more heat than carbon dioxide. Scientists continue to search for chemicals that could be used in place of CFCs and HFCs. Meanwhile, the future of the ozone layer remains in question.

LESS OZONE MEANS MORE UV RAYS

With less ozone in the atmosphere, more UV radiation has been reaching Earth. Scientists continue to study how increased UV radiation might be affecting life in the oceans near the North and South Poles. The base of the food web, the complex system by which organisms get food, is phyto-plankton, tiny plants and plantlike organisms. Tiny sea creatures feed on phytoplankton. The tiny creatures are food for larger sea creatures. If UV radiation damages the phytoplankton, the entire food web could be affected.

Increased UV radiation could also be linked to the problem of global warming. Most scientists believe that Earth's climate is growing warmer. They think the warming is caused by greenhouse gases that trap heat from

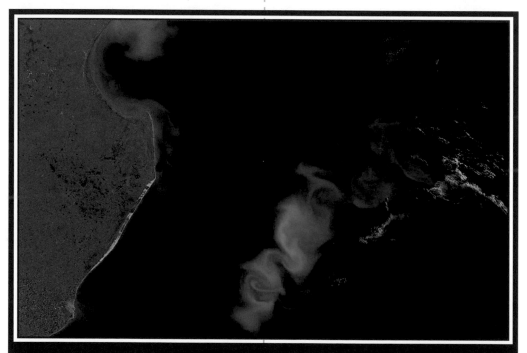

Phytoplankton (green blue) goes through stages of rapid reproduction. During these "blooms," the increase of phytoplankton results in much less carbon dioxide in the atmosphere.

the sun. The warming is melting ice on the Southern Ocean surrounding Antarctica. The ice floating on the ocean protects phytoplankton from the increased UV radiation reaching Earth because of the ozone hole. If global warming melts the slabs of ice, phytoplankton will lose that protection from UV radiation.

Slabs of ice on the ocean provide phytoplankton with shelter from UV rays. When the ice slabs melt and break apart, large amounts of phytoplankton die from the UV radiation.

Losing large amounts of phytoplankton could worsen global warming. Green plants and plantlike organisms make their own food with water, sunlight, and carbon dioxide (a major greenhouse gas) through a process called photosynthesis. The burning of coal, oil, and other fossil fuels sends carbon dioxide into the atmosphere. The phytoplankton in the oceans removes large amounts of carbon dioxide. Scientists fear that if the phytoplankton is damaged by UV radiation and no longer can remove carbon dioxide, even more carbon dioxide will build up in the atmosphere. This increase in greenhouse gas would make the global warming problem much worse.

UV INDEX FORECASTS DAILY DANGER

The amount of UV radiation reaching Earth varies from day to day. The intensity changes with changes in the ozone layer.

The National Weather Service and the Environmental Protection

Agency developed the UV Index, which is a daily forecast of the strength of UV radiation. Just as it is helpful to know how to dress for the weather, it is helpful to know how to dress for UV radiation.

UV INDEX

The UV Index uses a rating scale. For days predicted to have UV radiation at "very high" levels, the EPA issues a UV Alert.

Exposure Category	Index Number	Sun Protection Messages
LOW	2 or less	You can safely enjoy being outside. Wear sunglasses on bright days. If you burn easily, cover up and use sunscreen with an SPF of 15 or higher. In winter, reflection off snow can nearly double UV strength.
MODERATE	3–5	Take precautions if you will be outside, such as wearing a hat and sunglasses and using sunscreen with an SPF of 15 or higher. Reduce your exposure to the sun's most intense UV radiation by seeking shade during midday hours.
HIGH	6–7	Protection against sun damage is needed. Wear a wide-brimmed hat and sunglasses, use sunscreen with an SPF of 15 or higher, and wear a long-sleeved shirt and long pants when practical. Reduce your exposure to the sun's most intense UV radiation by seeking shade during mid-day hours.
VERY HIGH	8–10	Protection against sun damage is needed. If you have to be outside between 10 A.M. and 4 P.M., take steps to reduce sun exposure. A shirt, hat, and sunscreen are a must, and be sure you seek shade. Beachgoers should know that white sand and other bright surfaces reflect UV rays and can double UV exposure.
EXTREME	11 or more	Protection against sun damage is needed. If you have to be outside between 10 A.M. and 4 P.M., take steps to reduce sun exposure. A shirt, hat, and sunscreen are a must, and be sure you seek shade.

Source: The Environmental Protection Agency. www.epa.gov/sunwise/uvindex.html

GALAXY PORTRAIT REVEALS A BLAZE OF NEWBORN STARS

New Scientist
February 26, 2008

Newborn stars shine like celestial sparklers in a new portrait of the nearby Triangulum Galaxy—the most detailed ultraviolet image of a galaxy ever taken. Astronomers will use the image ... to create an "age map" of the galaxy's components to understand how galaxies evolve over time.

The Triangulum Galaxy ... lies about 2.9 million light-years from Earth and is a member of the "Local Group" of galaxies that includes the Milky Way.

"[I]t has a much higher star-formation rate than either the Milky Way or Andromeda," says image creator Stefan Immler of NASA's Goddard Space Flight Center in Greenbelt, Maryland. "All of this star birth lights up the galaxy in the ultraviolet."

Optical telescopes show objects in visible light. Astronomers use them to make images of the sun, moon, planets, and galaxies as human eyes would see them.

But there are other ways of seeing the universe. Stars and galaxies give off other kinds of electromagnetic radiation, including radio waves, X-rays, and ultraviolet light.

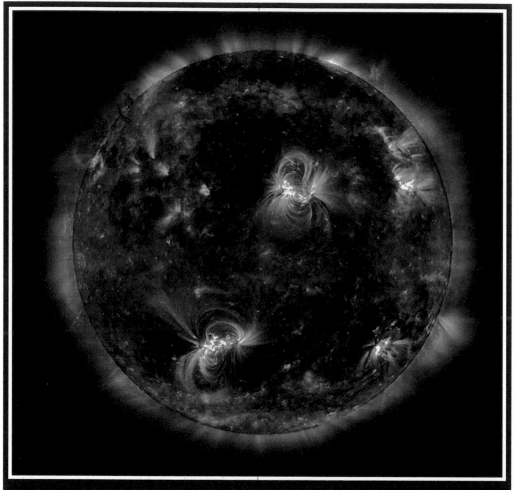

Using ultraviolet imaging, NASA recorded solar flares on the sun. Areas of the sun reached 1 million degrees Kelvin (1.8 million degrees Fahrenheit; 999,727 degrees Celsius).

Astronomers have created telescopes that detect these other types of radiation. Ultraviolet telescopes are useful for seeing very hot objects. Stars, for example, are made up of hot gases. The gases are especially hot when stars begin to form. Ultraviolet telescopes on satellites help astronomers study how and where stars are born. Closer objects, such as the sun and Earth, also give off or reflect ultraviolet light.

UVC RAYS KILL GERMS

The ozone layer in the atmosphere stops the sun's UVC rays, the UV rays with the shortest wavelength, from reaching Earth. Inventors have found a way to make artificial UVC rays that can kill disease-causing germs. The artificial UVC rays can damage DNA in bacteria, viruses, and molds.

Artificial UVC rays come from mercury vapor lamps. These lamps use the chemical element mercury

UV lights are used in scientific and medical labs for sterilization— a process of removing bacteria and germs from an area or object.

and an electric current to create UVC rays. The UVC rays destroy germs in water or air that moves past the mercury vapor lamps. UVC rays can be used in air conditioners, hospital operating rooms, and water purification systems.

UV RAYS IN "GREEN" LIGHTS

To save energy, many people began switching from incandescent to fluorescent lighting in the early 2000s. Fluorescent lighting uses less energy than ordinary, incandescent light bulbs. Incandescent lamps give off light when a thread-like filament made of the metal tungsten gets so hot that it glows. Incandescent lamps waste energy making heat.

Fluorescent lighting produces cool light.

It generates UV rays when electric current goes through mercury vapor sealed in tubes. The inside of each tube is lined with chemicals called

Fluorescent bulbs have become increasingly popular for outdoor lighting. They can last 10 to 15 times longer than incandescent bulbs.

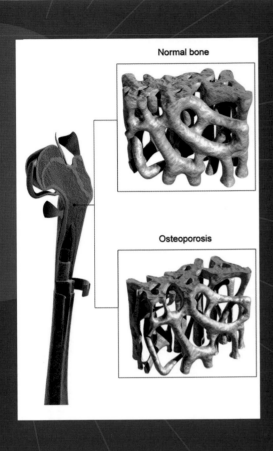

Normal bone

Osteoporosis

< OSTEOPOROSIS >

UVB rays cause skin to make vitamin D. Vitamin D helps your body get the right amount of calcium, a mineral needed for strong bones and teeth. A lack of vitamin D can cause such diseases as rickets and osteoporosis. Rickets creates soft, weak bones in children. Osteoporosis creates brittle, weak bones in older adults. But dermatologists warn people not to lie in the sun to let their skin make extra vitamin D. You can get all the UV rays you need just by going outside for 10 to 15 minutes three days a week. Many foods, such as milk, cheese, and fish, have vitamin D.

phosphors. UV rays strike the phosphors and cause them to give off light. The phosphors glow when they absorb the short-wavelength UV rays and give off longer-wavelength visible light rays. Because they are stopped by the phosphors, most UV rays cannot escape the tubes and cause harm.

UV RAYS CAN HELP FIGHT SKIN DISEASES

Even though UV rays can damage skin, they can also treat skin disorders. Dermatologists use UVA and UVB rays in a treatment called phototherapy. It is used in treating more than 40 skin disorders, including psoriasis.

Psoriasis is one of the most widespread skin disorders. Psoriasis causes red and swollen patches of dry skin. Some patches cover a small area of skin, while other patches cover almost the whole body. Psoriasis occurs when skin cells grow and die too fast. It normally takes a skin cell about a month to grow and die. In psoriasis, skin cells grow and die in about a week. As a result, the dead skin cells build up. Dermatologists treat psoriasis with drugs and ointments. Sometimes they beam ultraviolet rays onto the skin. Phototherapy slows the growth of skin cells.

The ultraviolet rays used in phototherapy, however, can cause skin problems. They can burn the skin, cause the skin to age, and lead to skin cancer. So researchers are looking for ways to fine-tune the UV rays given off

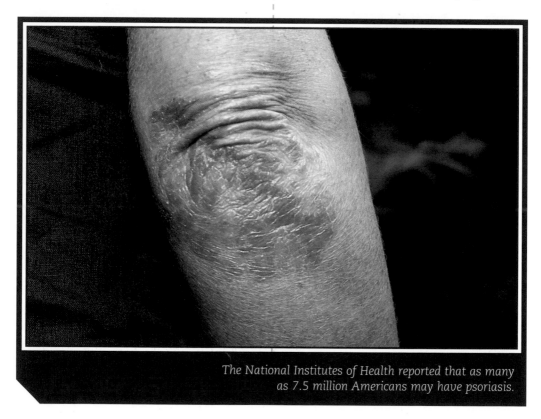

The National Institutes of Health reported that as many as 7.5 million Americans may have psoriasis.

A baby with jaundice was treated in a phototherapy chamber at a children's hospital in China. UV lights are used to eliminate a buildup of a substance called bilirubin in the child's blood.

by phototherapy machines. Researchers hope to find wavelengths of ultraviolet radiation that will do more good for human skin than harm.

Of all the rays that come from the sun, UV rays should be treated with the most caution. We need some UV radiation for good health. And artificial UV rays have many uses, from operating streetlights to cleaning air and sterilizing surgical instruments. Too much UV radiation, however, can be harmful or even deadly. When it comes to UV radiation, a good rule to follow is "Handle with care."

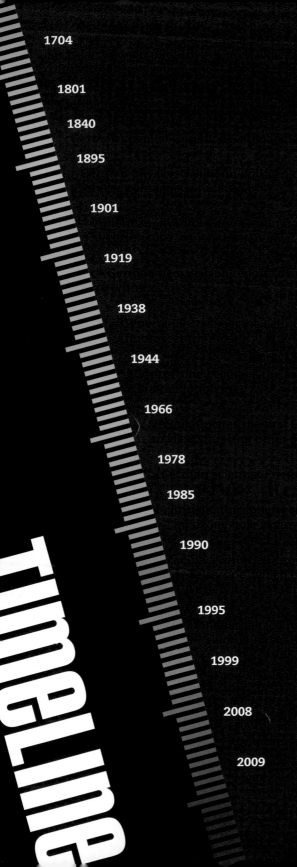

1704

1801

1840

1895

1901

1919

1938

1944

1966

1978

1985

1990

1995

1999

2008

2009

TimeLine

GLOSSARY

basal cell
type of skin cell in the epidermis

carcinogen
chemical, radiation, or other irritant that
can make cells become cancerous

cataract
cloudy area that forms in the lens
of the eye

cornea
clear covering in front of the eye

dermatologist
doctor who treats skin diseases
and disorders

dermis
layer of skin between the epidermis
and the subcutaneous tissue

epidermis
top layer of skin

gene
basic unit of heredity

greenhouse gases
gases in a planet's atmosphere that
trap heat energy from the sun

iris
colored circle in the center of the eye

melanin
dark pigment in skin cells

melanocyte
skin cell that makes melanin

melanoma
cancer that begins in a melanocyte

mole
bump or blemish on the skin

ozone
molecule made of three oxygen atoms; in
the atmosphere, ozone blocks UV rays

phosphor
solid substance that glows when exposed
to UV rays or other energy

phototherapy
medical treatment for skin problems
using UV rays

phytoplankton
mass of tiny plants and plantlike
organisms that live in the ocean

pigment
substance that gives color

prism
object, usually glass, that is cut to have
several triangular sides and can separate
white light into all colors

radiation
energy given off as electromagnetic
waves or subatomic particles

squamous cell
flat skin cells that provide the covering
for the body

wavelength
distance between two wave crests
(high points)

FURTHER RESOURCES

INTERNET SITES

FactHound offers a safe, fun way to find Internet sites related to this book. All of the sites on FactHound have been researched by our staff.

Here's all you do:

Visit *www.facthound.com*

FactHound will fetch the best sites for you!

FURTHER READING

Donovan, Sandy. *Stay Clear! What You Should Know About Skin Care.* Minneapolis: Lerner, 2009.

Gould, Alan, and Stephen Pompea. *Invisible Universe: The Electromagnetic Spectrum From Radio Waves to Gamma Rays.* Berkeley, Calif.: LHS GEMS, 2002.

Juettner, Bonnie. *Skin Cancer.* Detroit: Lucent Books, 2008.

Martins, John. *Ultraviolet Danger: Holes in the Ozone Layer.* New York: Rosen Publishing, 2007.

LOOK FOR OTHER BOOKS IN THIS SERIES:

Climate Crisis: The Science of Global Warming

Collapse!: The Science of Structural Engineering Failures

Cure Quest: The Science of Stem Cell Research

Feel the G's: The Science of Gravity and G-Forces

Goodbye, Gasoline: The Science of Fuel Cells

Great Shakes: The Science of Earthquakes

Nature Interrupted: The Science of Environmental Chain Reactions

Orbiting Eyes: The Science of Artificial Satellites

Out of Control: The Science of Wildfires

Recipe for Disaster: The Science of Foodborne Illness

Rise of the Thinking Machines: The Science of Robots

Storm Surge: The Science of Hurricanes

SOURCE NOTES

Chapter 1: "NV Town Posts Signal to Warn About UV Rays." *The Mercury News.* 28 Nov. 2008. 30 May 2009. www.mercurynews.com/news/ci_11095734?nclick_check=1

Chapter 2: Catherine Saint Louis. "Confused by SPF? Take a Number." *The New York Times.* 13 May 2009. 29 July 2009. www.nytimes.com/2009/05/14/fashion/14SKIN.html?_r=1&adxnnl=1&adxnnlx=1248881974-MPL8FkYNBrkXSIshJv/c9w

Chapter 3: Thomas H. Maugh II. "Tanning Beds As Carcinogenic As Asbestos and Cigarettes." *Los Angeles Times.* 28 July 2009. 29 July 2009. http://latimesblogs.latimes.com/booster_shots/2009/07/tanning-beds-as-carcinogenic-as-asbestos-and-radium.html

Chapter 4: Beth Whitehouse. "Children Should Wear Sunglasses When Outside." *Sun Sentinel.* 22 July 2009. 29 July 2009. www.sun-sentinel.com/health/family/sns-health-children-should-wear-sunglasses,0,2727699.story

Chapter 5: David A. Fahrenthold. "Chemicals That Eased One Woe Worsen Another." *The Washington Post.* 20 July 2009. 29 July 2009. www.washingtonpost.com/wp-dyn/content/article/2009/07/19/AR2009071901817.html

Chapter 6: Maggie McKee. "Galaxy Portrait Reveals a Blaze of New Stars." *New Scientist.* 26 Feb. 2008. 29 July 2009. www.newscientist.com/article/dn13380-galaxy-portrait-reveals-a-blaze-of-newborn-stars.html

ABOUT THE AUTHOR

Darlene R. Stille is a science writer and author of more than 80 books for young people. She grew up in Chicago and attended the University of Illinois, where she discovered her love of writing. She has received numerous awards for her work. She lives and writes in Michigan.

INDEX

actinic keratoses, 14
altitudes, 12
American Cancer Society, 21
artificial UV rays, 9, 14, 39,
    40, 43
astronomers, 37, 38–39

basal cell carcinoma, 20, 21, 28
basal cells, 19
bees, 8
blood, 12, 20, 22
"blue-blocker" sunglasses, 29
broad spectrum sunscreens, 15

cancer, 5, 12, 14, 18, 19, 20, 21,
    22, 24, 28, 29, 42
carbon dioxide, 30, 33, 35
carcinogens, 18, 19
cataracts, 27–28
Centers for Disease Control
    and Prevention, 20
chlorofluorocarbons (CFCs),
    30, 32–33
clouds, 13, 16, 32
colors, 6–7, 28–29
cones, 26
corneas, 25, 26, 27

daughter cells, 19
dermatologists, 10, 14, 15, 17,
    41, 42
dermis, 12

electromagnetic energy, 8–9,
    11, 38
electromagnetic spectrum,
    8–9
Environmental Protection
    Agency, 35–36
epidermis, 12, 13, 19, 21
equator, 12
eyes, 6, 7, 24, 25–28, 29, 38

first-degree sunburns, 13
fluorescent lighting, 40–41
food webs, 34

gamma rays, 9
German Aerospace Centre, 31
Gilchrest, Barbara A., 10
global warming, 30, 34–35
greenhouse gases, 30, 34–35

hydrofluorocarbons (HFCs),
    30, 33

Immler, Stefan, 37
insects, 8
International Agency for
    Research on Cancer, 18
iris, 25, 29

Lancet Oncology journal, 18
lenses, 25–26, 28–29

melanin, 13, 14, 29
melanocyte cells, 13, 22, 29
melanoma, 20, 22, 28
mercury vapor lamps, 39–40
microwaves, 8–9
Milky Way Galaxy, 37

National Cancer Institute, 20
National Weather Service,
    35–36
Newton, Sir Isaac, 6

osteoporosis, 41
ozone layer, 30, 31–33, 34, 35, 39

phosphors, 40–41
photokeratitis, 27
photosynthesis, 35
phototherapy, 41, 42–43
phytoplankton, 34, 35
prisms, 6–7
psoriasis, 41–42
pupils, 25

radio waves, 8–9, 38
rainbows, 6, 7
retina, 26
rickets, 41
rods, 26

Schiff, Steven, 24
search terms, 6
second-degree sunburns, 13
skin, 5, 11–14, 15, 17, 18, 19,
    20, 21, 22, 24, 29, 41–42, 43
snow blindness. *See*
    photokeratitis.
SPF (sun protection factor),
    10, 16–17, 23, 36
squamous cell carcinoma, 20,
    21, 28
subcutaneous tissue, 12, 13
sun, 4, 5, 9, 12, 13, 14, 16–17,
    27, 31, 32, 34–35, 36, 38,
    39, 43
sunblock, 15, 23
sunburns, 5, 10, 12–13, 14, 16,
    26, 27
sunglasses, 24, 25–27, 28–29, 36
sunscreen, 10, 11, 15–17, 23,
    24, 36

tanning, 12, 13–14, 18
telescopes, 38–39
third-degree sunburns, 13
titanium dioxide, 15
Triangulum Galaxy, 37
tumors, 20

UVA rays, 7, 11–12, 13–14, 15,
    18, 24, 28, 41
UVB rays, 7, 10, 11–13, 15, 16,
    17, 18, 24, 26–27, 28, 41
UVC rays, 7, 39–40
UV Index, 36

visible light, 6–7, 8, 25, 26, 38, 41
vitamin D, 41

warning lights, 4, 5
water, 13, 16, 27, 35, 40
wavelengths, 6–7, 8–9, 11, 12,
    39, 41, 43
World Health Organization, 18

X-rays, 8, 9, 38

zinc oxide, 15